dations

foundations

CESAR CASTELLANOS D.

DOCTRINE

LEVEL 1

TEACHERS' GUIDE

founda

G12
editors

CESAR CASTELLANOS D.© 2003
Published by G12 Editores
sales@g12bookstore.com

ISBN 1-932285-19-9

Made in Colombia

Printed in Colombia

CONTENTS

FORWARD

During my first seven years of training the church members for an effective ministeral job, I came to the conclusion that there were some things which needed improvement. One of them was in the way we were preparing our people. Though we were dedicated to give our Bible Institute students the best, we realized that after two years these students left with a wealth of biblical knowledge but without any clue of how to win people for Christ. I recall that after two years of having initiated the School of Leaders, I had a meeting with three of the students from the School of Leaders and one who had received his preparation through the Bible Institute asking them "How many cells do you have? And what is your occupation?".

One of the students responded, "I am in medical school and I have 90 cells." The other student replied, "I am studying to be a dentist, and I have 45 cells." The next student said, "I am studying medicine and I have 25 cells". Later the one who supposingly had greater knowledge of the Bible because he had been at the Bible Institute said, "I am an employee of a company and I have 3 cells".

That day I realized although the School of Leaders did not provide a wealth of information it did form efficient leaders; reason being we decided to stay with the leadership school. The result is seen by the fruit. Currently, we have more than 45.000 cells, as of January 2003, among men, women youth and children who meet once a week in the city of Bogotá.

Although this material was prepared to supply the need of apprenticeship for our church, Misión Carismática Internacional, we received witness by the Holy Spirit to share it with the communities who decided to implement the vision.

The material is not designed for the students to become theologians rather for them to have an effective tool to make disciples and to implement the vision.

I must express my gratitude to the editorial team in Bogotá and Miami for their valuable assitance. All of them have made it possible for this material to be a powerful tool in the hands of each student.

César Castellanos D.

Salvation

TEACHING OBJECTIVE

The student must understand the importance of salvation and the atoning work of Christ.

STUDENT OBJECTIVE

1 The student must be able to explain what grace is and what it is to be transformed by it.

2 The student must be able to explain why each person needs salvation.

BIBLICAL FOUNDATION
REFERENCE

John 3:16-21

CORRESPONDING
BIBLICAL
FOUNDATION

Ephesians 2:8-9

Acts 8:20

Genesis 6:5-8

Romans 3:20,24,28

Romans 10:4

Psalm 85:10-11

Romans 5:8

Romans 10:9-10

Romans 4:4-5

Philippians 4:13

Romans 7:14

Colossians 2:14

Galatians 6:14

1 Corinthians 1:30

KEY TEXT

"For God so loved the world
that he gave his one and only Son,
that whoever believes in him shall
not perish but have eternal life.
For God did not send his Son into
the world to condemn the world,
but to save the world through him".
John 3:16,17

PURPOSE

One day we were having dinner with a group of friends in a restaurant and the people at the table next to ours began to recount an experience that they had while crossing the mighty Magdalena River on a small boat. They talked about how the experience quickly turned deadly as the boat they were on capsized, throwing them into the waters leaving them floating about helplessly. At this point, they had almost no hope of being rescued, however one of them, out of desperation began to scream out for help with all of his might. Miraculously, God sent someone who helped them to be saved. Thanks to the wisdom of this man the travelers were rescued and were able to receive any necessary medical treatment.

- This experience illustrates the need mankind has to be rescued from the enslavement of sin. This condition leads him to a spiritual death and it does not allow him to enjoy the riches that God has destined for him.

- When God saw that man was lost, He decided to establish a plan to free him from the oppression of sin. The sacrifice of His own son, Jesus Christ, became necessary for this to be fulfilled.

- In this lesson you will see a clear picture of salvation, the reasons why to take hold of it and the role that the Son of God played in it. May all of this become a reality in your life as well as your family's.

1. ABUNDANT GRACE

We cannot negotiate our salvation. We cannot buy it or sell it (Ephesians 2:8-9). When Simon the magician offered Peter money to receive the anointing that the apostle had, Peter's answer was, «May your money perish with you, because you thought you could buy the gift of God with money» (Acts 8:20)

a. What is grace?

Grace God's mercy given to those who don't deserve it. It is the most amazing God-given gift to everyone who desires to receive it and it's priceless.

b. Description of Grace

Grace comes from the Greek term CARIS, which means beauty or attractiveness. Grace originates within God. He does not see us in our miserable condition. He always looks upon us favorably. This produces the miracle of transformation. A good example for this is the time when God decided to destroy the earth with a great flood because of man's wickedness and corrupt ways. The only thing that preserved mankind's existence was that "... Noah found favor in the eyes of the Lord" (Genesis 6: 5-8).

In his letter to the Romans, Paul said: "Therefore no one will be declared righteous in his sight by observing the law; rather, through the law we become conscious of sin (Romans 3:20). To that Paul adds "... and are justified freely by his grace through the redemption that came by Christ Jesus" (Romans 3:24).

Paul also reaffirmed to the Romans: "Christ is the end of the law so that there may be righteousness for everyone who believes" (Romans 10:4). This means that He grants to those who believe in Him what we sometimes want to achieve in our own strength.

The law made up part of the Word of God. It exposed divine righteousness in the people of Israel. But with Christ's death on the cross, the law died and grace was reborn. The psalmist said: "Love and faithfulness meet together; righteousness and peace kiss each other. Faithfulness springs forth from the earth and righteousness looks down from heaven" (Psalm 85:10-11).

God's severe righteousness is exact, fair and objective therefore it does not allow anything that is not perfect. When Jesus was on the cross, the proclamation that, "the sinner will die" met with the divine mercy that said: "But God demonstrates his own love for us in this: While we were still sinners, Christ died for us" (Romans 5: 8).

Indeed God had to punish the sinner but in His mercy, He chose to chastise His own Son instead, in order to save all lost humanity.

> Paul said: "For we maintain that a man is justified by faith apart from observing the law" (Romans 3:28).

> "Now when a man works, his wages are not credited to him as a gift but as an obligation. However, to the man who does not work but trusts God who justifies the wicked, his faith is credited as righteousness" (Romans 4:4-5).

Some people think that in order to yield their lives to the Lord they must first become better than what they already are, so they continue on their futile way, preparing, trying to convince themselves that, "tomorrow I will change." What is interesting about faith is that the Lord does not demand anything from us but our belief! Faith allows us to be able to declare that "All the chastisement that I, a sinner, deserved, fell on that man Jesus, who had committed no sin. And all the good that Jesus should have received came to me instead; just because I believed in Him. God looks at me through His Son, Jesus and I communicate with God through Jesus Christ as well."

By this grace we give Jesus all our weaknesses while we accept all His strength for ourselves:

· We surrender our sins and accept His salvation.
· We surrender our sicknesses and accept His healing.
· We surrender our needs and accept His provision.
· We surrender our anguish and accept His peace.
· We surrender our will and accept the guidance of the Holy Spirit.
· We surrender our human knowledge and accept His wisdom.

By grace we have absolute trust in the Lord Jesus Christ so we can say as Paul did: "I can do all things through Christ who strengthens me" (Philippians 4:13).

d. Grace and Sin

Paul said: "We know that the law is spiritual; but I am unspiritual, sold as a slave to sin" (Romans 7:14). Our problem is not that the law is spiritual. Our problem is that we have a carnal nature and we are slaves to sin.

In Rome, slaves were put up on a platform and placed against a post that had a spear nailed to it. This spear protruded over their heads as an indicator that that particular slave was for sale. Whoever bought the slave had total rights over him and the slave had no say at all; he could not chose who would buy him and become ruler and master over him.

The same thing happened to us because of sin. We were displayed in Satan's market and the spear over our head was the adversary's accusing finger. It was necessary for us to be bought by someone. That is why Jesus purchased us with His blood when He died on the cross.

The apostle Paul said: "having canceled the written decree, with its regulations, that was against us and that stood opposed to us; he took it away, nailing it to the cross" (Colossians 2:14). What is the written code or decree ? It is an accumulation of all the accusations that the adversary has recounted of the times that we walked in his territory. He uses it against us to capture us using a word said, a thought we had, or a negative situation that we experienced in the past; if we allow sin in our lives satan has that legal right. If we do not destroy every one of the arguments we have raised, taking them to the cross of Calvary, satan will continue to have that legal right because of sin (Revelations 12:10).

The cross is so powerful that the apostle Paul said: "May I never boast except in the cross of our Lord Jesus Christ, through which the world has been crucified to me, and I to the world" (Galatians 6:14).

2. WHAT IS SALVATION?

Salvation is equivalent to rescue.
As we use the term salvation, we are saying that a ransom will be exchanged, in order to set a person free from enslavement imposed on them by someone or something; it may even be because of a system or an oppressive situation. In this sense, salvation can be defined as redemption, which clearly implies that a price is to be paid for freedom to become a reality and for enslavement to disappear altogether.

Summary

Salvation is the process by which man is ransomed from the enslavement of sin through the atoning work of Jesus Christ on the cross of Calvary.

There are four parts to God's plan for salvation:

- Justification
- Regeneration
- Sanctification
- Redemption
  (Elaborate simply on each one).

"It is because of him that you are in Christ Jesus, who has become for us wisdom from God — that is, our righteousness, holiness and redemption" (1 Corinthians 1:30).

In order to receive regeneration we need:

- The permanent living Word of God (1 Peter 1:23)
- The work of the Holy Spirit (John 3:5-8)
- Faith in Jesus (Acts 3:16)

CONCLUSION

His saving grace is so precious that God, with all His power, could not find any other way to redeem us but through the blessed blood of his own Son. Thru Jesus everything that man lost in Paradise was restored back to him through faith. However, no man will be able to enjoy life and spiritual riches without first admitting his condition as a sinner, accepting Christ's sacrifice on the cross, and believing in Him.

APPLICATION

Examine your life thoroughly to see if there are any sinful ways that remain unconfessed to God. If there are any, renounce them and put forth every effort to live free from sin and embrace a life of salvation that has been planned just for you.

EVALUATION

You can develop a questionnaire that will evaluate the student's personal experiences as it relates to the indicators in this lesson.

RECOMMENDATIONS

Biblical

Study in depth this subject in the Bible.

Methodological

Use interaction as you teach this lesson.

Bibliography

As Firm As The Rock, series by Pastor Cesar Castellanos

STUDENTS´ ASSIGNMENT

Make a list of people who are close to you, such as relatives or acquaintances that have not yet opened their hearts to Jesus. Pray for them and ask the Lord for an opportunity where by you can share the plan of salvation with them, so that they can also share in God's Grace.

1 Questionnaire for further study

1. The need for man's salvation arose with the first couple, Adam and Eve,_____ against God.

God's requirement for salvation is revealed in Genesis 2:16b, 17. According to this text they could_____, but they should not _____; disobedience would cause the _____ of man.

2. The role of Jesus as Savior is called atoning work. Look up the meaning of the term atonement and write out its definition in the space provided.

_____

_____

3. According to Hebrews 9:12, the atoning work of Jesus was fulfilled through the

_____

_____

4. Justification means to declare someone as righteous. According to Romans 3:24 we are justified by _____ and according to Titus 3:7 we are justified by grace in order to become _____

5. We can maintain our salvation as long as we continue in holiness. That is, separated to God and from the world. Fill in the next text in relation to this: 1 John 2:15-17

"Do not love the world, _____. If anyone loves the world, _____ _____. For everything in the world—the cravings of sinful man, the lust of his eyes and the boasting of what he has and does, _____ , _____. The world and its desires pass away, but the man who does the will of God _____."

6. 1 Thessalonians 5:23 implies that holiness is produced in us by the work of _____.

7. Being completely holy consists of _____,
_____ , and _____ 1 Thessalonians 5: 23.

8. One of the effects of salvation is regeneration.
Based on John 3: 3-5, explain in your own words how
regeneration takes place_____
_____

9. Why is it said that Jesus was made a curse for us? Give a clear answer based on Galatians 3: 13
_____
_____

10. Specify the three areas that redemption is comprised of according to the following bible references:

Romans 6:20-22 _____

Isaiah 53:6 _____

Isaiah 53:4,5 _____

Corinthians 8:9 _____

The New Birth

LESSON

TEACHING OBJECTIVE

The student must understand and experience the New Birth.

STUDENT OBJECTIVE

1 The student must be able to define the Old and New Nature.

2 The student must be able to explain what New Birth is.

3 The student must be able to explain how someone can be born again.

John 3:1-6

John 10:10b

Ephesians 4:17-24

James 1:18

John 6:63

John 15:3

John 1:12,13

2 Corinthians 1:22

Ephesians 1:13

Isaiah 1:6

2 Corinthians 5:17

KEY TEXT

In reply Jesus declared, "I tell you the truth, no one can see the kingdom of God unless he is born again".
John 3:3

PURPOSE

My mother used to have contstant problems with one of my brothers who was rebellious and had absolutely no interest in changing his ways; any effort that was made toward positive change yielded, to contrary results more rebellion. One day however, he showed up at church and when I looked at him I noticed a different look in his eyes; his countenance was different. He approached me and said, "I am a Christian now, Jesus lives in me. You know that I have been rebellious and violent but Jesus has changed me; some days ago I prayed to Him and said, 'Jesus I am not going to do anything to change. If you want to save me, do it by yourself, I'm not going to help you in any way.' And before I finished praying, I felt as if a very powerful light consumed me, leaving me face down, flat on the floor. I was almost unconscious! Then I turned and saw myself; my old self peel away from me as if it was some despicable costume that I had been wearing. It was my old nature leaving from me. The voice of the Lord then spoke to me and said, 'now I am going to walk with you, but you have to do whatever I command you to do'."

From that moment on, my brother became a source of inspiration for many who did not believe that God could change a person's life.

When man lives according to his misdeeds and sins, his actions are prompted by his old nature; his understanding is darkened and his heart is hardened so that he develops a behavior which opposes God's will.

When an individual realizes that he is a sinner, it is his heart's desire to be set free for this enslavement. He wants to experience a new life. He has recognized his need to go through the process of the New Birth, as described for us in the Bible.

1.WHAT IS THE NEW BIRTH?

It is an experience that one has when he accepts Christ in his heart as the only sufficient Savior. When a person has separated himself from God because of sin, even though he remains in touch with the external world and is aware of his state, his spiritual nature remains dead. When one open his heart to Jesus his spiritual life begins to flow with life because Jesus said: "I have come that you may have life and have it more abundantly" (John 10:10b).

The New Birth is a spiritual regeneration that guarantees that man will be admitted in God's kingdom. In other words, nobody can call himself a Christian, let alone enter into God's kingdom, through works of his own flesh (personal efforts) if he has not been born again from above.

2. WHAT DOES THE NEW BIRTH CONSIST OF?

Jesus told Nicodemus: "I tell you the truth, no one can see the kingdom of God unless he is born again" (John 3:3).

When Jesus died on the cross of Calvary, he offered himself as a sacrifice for the restoration and redemption of all mankind. This opened a door for him to live and experience a new life set apart from the world's contaminations such as curses, spiritual, physical and material poverty and all the burdens that are oppressive to man.

Jesus made sure that Nicodemus clearly understood that every human being, regardless of his social, economic or cultural condition, must allow the Lord to transform his old nature into a new one designed according to God's purpose.

a.   The Role of the Word in the New Birth

"He chose to give us birth through the word of truth, that we might be a kind of first fruits of all he created" (James 1:18). When a person receives the Word of God, breath of life from the Holy Spirit is received as well. The Lord Jesus said: "The Spirit gives life; the flesh counts for nothing. The words I have spoken to you are spirit and they are life" (John 6:63).

The Word of God that washes the inner part of each person bestowing upon him, new life (Ephesians 5:26; John 15:3).

b.   The role of the Holy Spirit in the New Birth

Together with the Word, the Holy Spirit intervenes specifically in the process of the New Birth.

"Yet to all who received him, to those who believed in his name, he gave the right to become children of God — children born not of natural descent, nor of human decision or a husband's will, but born of God" (John 1:12,13).

When we are born again the Holy Spirit plants the life of Christ in us. He will also be in charge of sealing it so that it will not be revoked, guaranteeing for us eternal life. (2 Corinthians 1:22; Ephesians 1:13)

3. OLD MAN AND NEW NATURE

Think of a man with a worn out vehicle for a moment. He wants to purchase a new one but doesn't have the money to do so. Let's say that he happens to run across a car salesman who has been looking for him and says, "Sir, I have the solution for you. Just give me your old car and I will give you this new Mercedes-Benz free of charge."

Of course anyone would say, "This is the best business deal in the world!" A deal like that is quite beneficial, not to mention profitable. However, God made a better deal by casting away all our ills bringing us complete restauration and goodness in his Son Jesus Christ.

a. Old man

New Birth has to do with leaving the old man totally behind in order to enjoy a new nature. ">From the sole of your foot to the top of your head there is no soundness - only wounds and welts and open sores, not cleansed or bandaged or soothed with oil" (Isaiah 1:6).

This is the description of our old condition or old nature, which also implies acting according to the desires of the flesh (Galatians 5:19-21).

b. New nature

When you leave the old man behind, all the sinful burdens that came along with it and then you receive Jesus as Lord and Savior, He puts a new garment on you and fills you with His presence, giving you a new nature according to His character and purpose. "Therefore, if anyone is in Christ, he is a new creation; the old has gone, the new has come!" (2 Corinthians 5:17).

CONCLUSION

The Christian life is the best life on earth to live! Through it, you can experience genuine happiness if you fulfill just one requirement: Do not step onto the enemy's grounds. Yes, God gives us everything we need but He demands that we surrender everything that we are to Him.

If someone desires to be known as a Christian and to enter into God's kingdom to enjoy the heritage of eternal life, he must experience the New Birth that consists of giving up being led by the desires of the flesh and living according to the leading of the Holy Spirit through faith in God's Word.

APPLICATION

In your New Birth experience, never forget the words that Jesus spoke to Nicodemus and always count on the Holy Spirit to help inspire you in your new life.

Share with someone about what is to be born again. Talk about how you lived under influence of your old self. Give examples of how you now have the fruit of the Spirit.

TIME OF MINISTRY

Minister to the students, encourage them to examine their lives and see if they still act, or react according to the old nature, and lead them to renounce in prayer to all of the sins listed in Ephesians 4:25-32.

EVALUATION

At the end of the class, have a time of questions and answers. Determine the students´ comprehension of the lessons.

RECOMMENDATIONS

Biblical

In order to be sure that the points brought out in this lesson are accomplished, it is important to accurately interpret and explain the biblical passages covered because this lesson contains very significant theological concepts.

Methodological

A role-play depicting segments taught this far would be a good way to measure the student's comprehension of the lessons.

Bibliographical

As **Firm As The** Rock, Series by Pastor Cesar Castellanos

STUDENTS' ASSIGNMENT

Make a list specifying areas in your life that are still part of the old nature and confront them with the Word. What does God say about them ?

2 Questionnaire for Further Study

1.   According to Ephesians 4:17-19 write down six characteristics of the old self.

They walk in the _____
They have a _____
Separated from _____ because of
_____ Being ignorant due to _____
Having lost all sensitivity, they have given themselves to

_____

_____

So as to indulge in _____

_____

Remember that the old man (old nature) implies walking according to the desires of the flesh, and that the new nature emerges when man opens his heart to Jesus allowing him to dwell in his inner being. Here begins a spiritual revival that transforms the human being's behavior.

2. Why do we have to put off our old man? Ephesians 4:22.

_____

_____

3. Describe the new man, Ephesians 4:24.

_____

4. Make a list of the works of the flesh, Galatians 5:19-21.

_____

5. Specify the fruit of the Spirit, Galatians 5:22.

_____

6.   How should we present our bodies? Romans 12:1.

_____

7. What do we prove by renewing our mind? Romans 12:2

_____

8. How many righteous ones, who understand and seek God, are there? Romans 3:10-11.

_____

_____

9. What is the worth of the ones who turn away? Romans 3:12.

_____

"X" marks the correct answer.
According to Romans 3:12-13 the throats of the evil ones are compared to:

a. A merchant's ship from afar ( )
b. A lighted torch   ( )
c. Open graves   ( )

What is found under deceitful lips?

a. Flattering words   ( )
b. Some wickedness   ( )
c. Poisonous vipers   ( )

11. What are the evil ones mouth full of? Romans 3:14.

_____

_____

The True Repentance

LESSON

TEACHING OBJECTIVE

The student must understand repentance as the only way to restore our relationship with God.

STUDENT OBJECTIVE

1   The student must be thoroughly acquainted with The Parable of the Lost Son.

2   The student must be able to explain the attitude that we must have toward sin.

BIBLICAL FOUNDATIONAL
REFERENCE

Luke 15:11-32

CORRESPONDING
BIBLICAL
FOUNDATION

Romans 5:12

Romans 1:21-25

Romans 3:16-18

Genesis 3:10

Psalm 51

Matthew 27:3-5

Psalms 32:5

1 John 1:9

Galatians 3:13

Colossians 2:14-15

KEY TEXT

"...How many of my father's hired
men have food to spare, and here I
am starving to death! I will set out
and go back to my father and say to
him: Father, I have sinned against
heaven and against you.
I am no longer worthy to be called
your son; make me like one of your
hired men. So he got up and went
to his father..."
Luke 15:17-20

PURPOSE

A 46 year old man named Antonio desparately wanted to make an appointment with me. I agreed and we met in my office. In that moment as he entered my office, he began to cry uncontrollably, pouring out his heart. He lamented, "I feel guilty because of the deaths of my two daughters. They were 3 and 5 years old. I know I have failed God by allowing improper relationships into my life and now I feel that I am the most miserable person on earth" He continued to tell me about his story. He was shopping in a store in a town near Bogotá, and for a moment he took his eyes off of his daughters. Through his own carelessness, he did not notice that they had gone out of the store and into the traffic riddled street where they were both struck down by a car with failed brakes. The two girls died instantly. "This has been the most devastating trauma of my life," Antonio cried. "I wish with all my heart that I could go back in time to have my daughters again to take better care of them. Ever since this happened, I have been grieving and crying. It is my own fault that I no longer have my girls here with me."

This was a very traumatic situation. Through it I could see a very clear picture of repentance reflected in this man's life.

· Admitting the fault.
· Being deeply sorrowed due to having failed.
· Wishing time to go backwards not to fail again.
· Begging for a second chance.

God is merciful. Through His son, Jesus Christ, He comes to those who have experienced similar situations like that of Antonio's. He is ready to aid all those who are truly willing to admit their sins and to free us out of such enslavement. God offers reconciliation to the same degree that you are repentant before Him.

1.WHAT IS REPENTANCE?

It is not a feeling but a decision of your will, followed by ordained action. In the original Greek, repentance is a change of mind. We must change our thoughts, attitudes and feelings. Repentance is feeling a deep sorrow for having offended God and seeing sin as God does.

Until the Holy Spirit, who works in us, to show us the magnitude of how sinful and wicked we really are, it is impossible to practice true repentance.

Repentance then, must be understood as the process in which an individual has committed a wrongful act; and then humbles his heart completely admitting that he has failed the Almighty. Repentance implies, not only admitting the mistake, but making the firm decision to not do it again.

When you are repentant, you are not prompted by your feelings alone. >From the depths of your soul you have decided that you could not withstand the pain of causing the Holy Spirit grief anymore so you agree to lay aside all that would grieve Him. Your life now has a totally new meaning.

In the Hebrew language, the word used to express repentance is "metamelomai",implying a feeling of wanting to change a behavior. In the Greek the word is "epistrophe" which means to turn to, or making a "U" turn. Repentance is turning your back on sin and turning your face to God. It is a change of the mindset. (Romans 12:2).

2. REPENTANCE FROM THE PRODIGAL SON'S PERSPECTIVE

The story of the Prodigal Son in Luke 15: 11-32 is one of the most perfect and impressive pictures of repentance. The story is about a wealthy father who had two sons. One day the younger son asked the father for his share of the estate to do as he pleased with it. The father agreed to give it to him. The son went about his way spending it with friends so much so that he ended up in a state of squander. All he had was wasted away leaving him no choice to work as a laborer feeding pigs.

"In the midst of his unbearable situation, he came to his senses and said, 'How many of my father's hired men have food to spare, and here I am starving to death! I will set out and go back to my father and say to him, 'Father, I have sinned against heaven and against you. I am no longer worthy to be called your son; make me like one of your hired men'. So he got up and went to his father" (Luke 15:17-20).

What this well-known prodigal son did was make an inner vow to change his outer behavior. It was the act of repentance that drove him to prove himself to God, to himself and to all those who had been affected by his misbehavior.

a. THE SON'S ATTITUDE

Here listed are four points that expressed his true repentance:

1. He stopped along the way to reflect on his present condition.

2. He renewed his mind and decided to ask for a second chance.

3. He decided in his own will to go back to his father.

4. He made the desicion to confess his sins to this father.

The list below typifies the attitude of the good father who has his arms open, ready to receive us in the heavenly place, once we return to him, (Luke 15:20-24).

1. He sees the son from afar ("But while he was still a long way off, his father saw him.").
2. He is moved with compassion ("... and was filled with compassion for him.").
3. He ran to meet him ("...he ran to his son, threw his arms around him and kissed him.").
4. He has a garment of righteousness prepared ("But the father said to his servants, `Quick! Bring the best robe and put it on him'.").
5. He restores the son's authority ("... Put a ring on his finger.").
6. He entrusts the son with the biggest ministry - preaching the gospel ("...and sandals on his feet.").

CONCLUSION

Everyone who desires to have a relationship with the Father and enjoy His blessings must have experienced genuine repentance and an understanding that there is a heartfelt sorrow for having offended God, and a real willingness of heart to take on a new direction on life, changing your mind and behavior.

APPLICATION

Make a list of the sinful actions that you thought you had overcome but are still hindrances in your life. Express a deep sorrow for having committed them. Confess them to the Lord and renounce them, breaking every curse, in the name of Jesus Christ.

Explain what true repentance is to someone and help him, through your own experience, to take the necessary steps for him to enjoy the blessing of God's forgiveness.

TIME OF MINISTRY

According to the lesson theory, guide your students to restoration with God if they have failed.

EVALUATION

Applying the concepts and ministering to the student, make up a good method of evaluation.

RECOMMENDATIONS

Methodological

A questionnaire may be useful to carry out the development of the subject.

Bibliography

In order to achieve a better development of the subject, it is necessary to read the book Repentance: Entrance Door for the Blessing, from the Series, "As Firm As The Rock" by Pastor Cesar Castellanos.

STUDENTS' ASSIGNMENT

Analyze cases A and B and answer:

a. How would a non Christian person come to repentance? (Write down a specific case)

b. How would a Christian person in sin come to repentance? (Write down a specific case)

3 Questionnaire for Further Study

1. List three things that happen to the person that is in Christ, 2 Corinthians 5:17.

_____

_____

_____

2. List the three things that every man must do, Isaiah 55:6-8.

_____

_____

3. What is God's commandment to every man? Acts 17:30.

_____

_____

4. What did people do after being baptized? Mark 1:4.

_____

5. Acts 2:37-38, which promises did Peter say they would receive if they repented and were baptized?

_____

_____

_____

6. What should the different groups, coming to be baptized in water, do? Luke 3:1014.

_____

7. Whoever believes and is baptized will be saved, but whoever does not believe will be condemned. (Mark 16:16) Who would be saved? _____

_____

_____

8. Who can forgive? Mark 2:7.

_____

9. What happens if we confess our sins? 1 John 1:9.

_____

_____

10. Who are the ones that prosper? Proverbs28:13.

_____

_____

11. In addition to confessing our sins, whose sins must we confess? Leviticus 26:40.

_____

_____

12. List three things that David did for the Lord to forgive him, Psalm 32:5.

_____

_____

Bible Institute

LESSON

TEACHING OBJECTIVE

The student should understand the reasons why the Bible is the Word of God and the foundation for Christian life.

STUDENT OBJECTIVE

1   The student should understand the need to know the Bible as the foundation for Christian life.

2   The student should mention the biblical structure and its characteristics.

BIBLICAL FOUNDATIONAL REFERENCE

2 Timothy 3:16-17

CORRESPONDING BIBLICAL FOUNDATION

2 Peter 1:19-20

Acts 13:16-40

1 John 2:21

John 14:9

John 16:13

2 Peter 1:20

1 Peter 2:2

1 Peter 1:25

Isaiah 55:11

KEY TEXT

"All Scripture is God breathed and is useful for teaching, rebuking, correcting and training in righteousness, so that the man of God may be thoroughly equipped for every good work".
2 Timothy 3:16-17

Purpose

It is important to recognize that as Christians we have the need to share Christ to others and take them to His feet. Many times we do not have the foundation to tear down the mental and spiritual arguments that the persons have because we do not have the basic knowledge of the Word of God.

Each one of the truths that are in the scriptures take us to a profound knowledge of God and it is through this that we can be firm on Christ the rock.

Like those men who had to pass the same test, one was sustained victoriously by the solid foundation of the sacred scriptures and passed the test. The other one did not sustain himself because he had no foundation therefore his life ended in failure, (Matthew 7:24-27).

The reason why you need to know the "Word" is to lead a life of success, fullness, and to fulfill the purpose of God. You will receive peace, trust, wisdom, correction and victory to confront difficulties and adversities.

Today more than ever I invite you to enjoy the promises for you that are contained in the Word of God, which is the Bible.

Only in the Word of God can the believer find the authority in order to be justified by faith.

1.What is the Bible?

The word "Bible" comes from the Greek "Biblos" which means books. It was considered that these writings, on their own, made up a concrete and defined group of works that were superior to any other literary works in existence. The Bible is known as the Sacred Scriptures, containing that which elevates it to the category of the book of excellence.

The New Illustrated Biblical Dictionary points out the fact that the Bible is not merely a book, but a compound of many books. The use of the term scripture illustrates an important fact; that although they were written by a diversity of writers they present a marvelous unity that reveals a logical order that has not ceased for thousands of years.

The Bible can be defined as the sacred book that contains the Word of God written by many different authors under the revelation of the Holy Spirit.

2.Importance of the Bible

a. For it contains the word of God and the revelation of Christ.
b. For it contains the divine laws.
c. For its historical diffusion; compiles 66 books which are the summary of over 40 writers throughout the ages.

3. Aspects which distinguish the Bible from other books

The Bible is the registry of the divine revelation for man, that is to say God is the main author. Its ultimate purpose is the salvation of man. The Bible contains the truth and there are no mistakes in it. The purpose of the Bible is to provide instruction and to lead man to the knowledge that Jesus is the only way to the Father, therefore the only way by which we can be saved.

These are some features that distinguish the Bible from other books:

a. The revelation of God to man

Originally this revelation was transmitted orally from generation to generation and then in written form in Hebrew, Aramaic, and Greek. Little by little it has been brought to a great part of humanity.

b. In reference to the salvation of man

The unity of the Bible, as will be noticed later, consists of the fact that all of its contents bring forth the following:

1. It introduces the person who brings salvation, that is to say God through Jesus Christ.

2. It indicates the way in which salvation can be obtained, which is by the Grace of God, who demands a public confession of faith in His Son and obedience to His Word.

3. It states who receives salvation: those who through faith in Jesus, have become the people of God or the church of Christ (Acts 13:16-40).

A fundamental aspect of the Bible is that it reveals the truth about life that man so longs to know. In the Holy Bible God shows that the truth about the existence and the destiny of man goes beyond earthly limits. Only He, in His omniscience and sovereignty, can make it known to man.

Taking into account the truth that God makes known through the Scriptures, all possibility of error are reduced to nothing. The Lord Jesus Christ Himself, making reference to the truth, that was longed for and needed by humanity, said to His disciples in a closing prayer:

"Sanctify them by the truth; your word is truth" (John 17:17).

Throughout history the Word of God enclosed in the Bible has been proved and has been able to come forward, overcoming every attack, confirming the words of John the apostle:

"I do not write to you because you do not know the truth, but because you do know it and because no lie comes from the truth." (1 John 2:21)

d. Jesus as the main character

Throughout the 66 books that make it up, the Bible makes reference to the instrument used by God to give salvation to man: Jesus Christ. This is continually declared and manifested in the Old Testament.

It is the person of Jesus Christ that allows the cohesion and the unity of the biblical writings. In making reference to the plan of salvation the Holy Scriptures are clear. They indicate that salvation would only be effective through Jesus Christ; His ministry, His sacrifice on the Cross of Calvary and H is resurrection to justify humanity before the Father. Jesus is described in the Scriptures as the only way to God. That is why He Himself said:

"Anyone who has seen me has seen the Father" (John 14:9b).

4. Basic Structure of the Bible

Historical and biographical books

These include the books from Genesis to Esther including Leviticus. They state historical facts about the way in which God progressively revealed Himself and His truth.

Books of the Law

They include Leviticus, parts of Exodus, Numbers, and Deuteronomy. Its contents exhibit the laws given to the people of Israel in the time they lived among the pagan nations.

Books of Poetry and Wisdom

From Job to the Songs of Solomon Hebrew poetry is evident in these books. They cover various subjects, especially the book of Proverbs which express principles for individual and social development.

Prophetic Books

These are the books from Isaiah to Malachi. These books written long ago, tell about future events of history.

The Gospels

The first four books of the New Testament. Mathew through John tell about the life of Jesus, including His birth, ministry, teachings, miracles, sufferings, death, resurrection and ascension.

Book of Acts

It contains the history of Christianity from the first century and it points out how the good news of salvation through Christ was accepted by Jews and Gentiles.

The Epistles

Starting with the book to the Romans, ending in the book of Jude, are the letters addressed specifically to the churches of that era, as well as their leaders. They were written to tutor the new churches in the Christian Faith and to set divine parameters.

The Book of Revelation

This book demonstrates the divine plans for the end times in a symbolic way. It constitutes a specific message to the churches of the first century and to the believers of all ages. It talks basically about future events.

5. Some Characteristics of the Bible

Illumination
Inspiration
Revelation
Exactitude
Unity
Interest wide spread throughout history and the World
Actuality, Is for our days
Preservation
Fulfilled prophecies

CONCLUSION

It is very fundamental to understand the importance of this book for your life; don't stay ignorant of what the Word says about you. The most important thing is that by reading it you will be strengthened spiritually so you may strengthen others.

APPLICATION

If you have not read it all, set a goal to read it in an orderly fashion, analyze it and meditate upon it.

EVALUATION

A quiz can be useful to evaluate the proposed indicators. Review the structure of the Bible with the students.

RECOMMENDATIONS

Bibliographical

For a better development of the topic it is necessary to consult the book "Knowing the Truth" by Pastor Cesar Castellanos, "Panorama of the Bible" by Macquay Eral, "Introduction to the Bible" by Demarrar Donald

Methodological

It is recommended to have a combination of discussion, and questions and answers, as well as an applied workshop.

STUDENTS´ ASSIGNMENT

Learn the order of all the books of the Bible to be better able to handle it.

Have the student research the features presentations on point number 5 of this class.

4 Questionnaire for Further Study

PLEASE COMPLETE:

1. The Bible is: _____
   _____
   _____

2. Why is the Bible a sacred book? _____
   _____

3. What is the importance of the Bible? _____
   _____

4. Explain which is the central topic of the Bible? _____
   _____

5. Which is the basic scripture of the Bible? _____
   _____

6. Biblically define the following characteristics of the Bible:

Inspiration _____
Revelation _____
Preservation _____
Fulfilled Prophesies _____
Interest _____
Up-to-date _____
Unity _____
Exactitude _____

Prayer

LESSON

TEACHING OBJECTIVE

The student must understand and apply the 10 levels of prayer.

STUDENT OBJECTIVE

1   The student must explain the reason why Jesus' teaching about the Lord's Prayer was so important.

2   The student must explain the levels of prayer.

BIBLICAL FOUNDATIONAL REFERENCE

Mathew 6:5-15

CORRESPONDING BIBLICAL FOUNDATION

Hebrews 10:22

Matthew 23:25,26

Isaiah 26:20

James 4:3

2 Chronicles 7:14

John 4:23

Psalm 32 y 51

Nehemiah 1

John 16:24

Psalm 100:4

KEY TEXT

"But when you pray, go into your room, close the door and pray to your Father, who is unseen. Then your Father, who sees what is done in secret, will reward you".
Matthew 6:6

PURPOSE

Undoubtedly, prayer is the only means that God has established to change lives, families, cities, nations and continents. If God's people really knew how to pray, our governments would be founded on the truth of the gospel of Jesus Christ, committed and fighting for people's social welfare. Throughout all history we find that simple men were able to believe in God and by their prayers their nations were transformed. They reconciled the people with God and brought a spiritual awakening.

The Lord never taught his disciples how to preach, but He did teach them how to pray. He gathered them and said «This is how you should pray.» And He gave them simple and precise directions about the way they should develop effective prayer. If you are a disciple of Christ you must learn how to communicate with God.

An example is the fact that you have a specific key that lets you into the door of your home when you arrive everyday. Well, prayer is the master key that opens the door and allows you to commune with God and have direct relationship with Him.

The purpose of this lesson is to teach the levels of prayer thoroughly, so that the student can communicate with God and have the windows of heaven open so that God's abundant blessings can be poured out upon the student's life.

THE TEN LEVELS OF PRAYER

Besides showing us how to attain effective praying, the Lord, Jesus Christ, gave us the Lord's prayer as a model to communicate with God, not as a structure of vain repetitions, but as a guide with specific levels that embrace every need of daily human life.

1. Level of Redemption – 'Our Father'

No one can call God "Father" if he has not been redeemed by Jesus' blood. Jesus could call God "Father" because he had God's same divine nature. For us to be able to do the same, we must be adopted as children of God, which we can achieve by having faith in Jesus Christ (John 1:12-13).

2. Level of authority – 'in heaven'

Through prayer we recognize that the heavens are God's throne. It is believed that the apostle Paul was carried away to the third heaven (God's heaven) and that is the reason why in Ephesians 1:17-18 The apostle longs for us as believers to understand the hope we have been called to, the riches in glory of Christ Jesus, the inheritance we have acquired as saints and His incomparably great power for us who believe. This power raised Christ from the dead and seated him at His right hand in the heavenly places (Ephesians 1:19 -23).

3. Level of worship – 'Hallowed be your name'

God's nature is holy, that is, completely separated from wickedness. Everything He created was made with the purpose of worshiping and glorifying Him. That is the reason why Jesus said to the Samaritan woman that the Father seeks worshipers who worship in Spirit and in truth (John 4:23-24).

4. Level of government - 'Your kingdom come'

God has established a government plan. When we understand this, it fulfills God´s divine purpose for our lives. We must accept it and spread it throughout the earth. It begins with a person who grasps it, then gets his family involved (the latter involves other families) until it is established in every social arena. Society is the one in charge of choosing the representatives who make major decisions on govermental level (Proverbs 29:2). This is the way to have godly people as authorities.

5. Level of evangelism – 'your will be done on earth as it is in heaven'

God's will is that none should perish, but that all turn to him in repentance (John 6:39). Our commitment must be to spread the manifestation of God's love through his son Jesus Christ, throughout the world. We do this by sharing the Good News of salvation with those who are lost.

6. Level of provision – 'Give us today our daily bread'

It is God's plan that his children prosper spiritually, physically and financially. That is why John the apostle said to Gaius: "Dear friend, I pray that you may enjoy good health and that all may go well with you, even as your soul is getting along well" (3 John 2).

7. Level of forgiveness – 'Forgive us our debts, as we also have forgiven our debtors'

When we pray without having experienced God's forgiveness in our lives, and without having granted forgiveness to those who have offended us, our prayer has no power, because the lack of forgiveness becomes a barrier between God and us (Matthew 5:23-24).

8. Level of protection – 'And lead us not into temptation'

Man is in constant danger day after day. Temptation is always near trying to capture him. His only escape is a strict (disciplined) life of prayer where he is seeking God's protection to keep him far away from danger (Proverbs 22:3; 1 Corinthians 6:18).

9. Level of deliverance – 'But deliver us from the evil one'

There are two forces that operate in the spirit realm: good and evil. A person that experienced the new birth has passed from darkness to light, but must constantly ask God, in prayer, to deliver him from sicknesses, accidents, plagues, poverty, etc. God has promised to shower us with blessings depending on our attitude towards His Word (Deuteronomy 28; Psalm 144:2).

10. Level of safety – "For yours is the kingdom and the power and the glory forever"

The most stable and lasting safety that God has given us is Jesus Christ. Although Jesus died in weakness, he rose again in power and obtained authority in the heavens and in the earth therefore all things are submitted under his feet. He is the one who gives us assurance and trust (John 10:27-28).

CONCLUSION

Prayer is the means provided by God for every believer to establish an intimate relationship with Him. It is through our fervent prayers that we can open the doors of heaven for the blessings to be abundantly poured out upon our lives. A prayer life must be disciplined since every Christian depends continually on the Father.

APPLICATION

Determine in your heart to make prayer your lifestyle; something inherent to your personality. In order to do that:

- Choose a specific daily hour.
- Select a specific place.
- Use the Bible as your support.
- Journalize the things the Lord has revealed to you according to your petitions.

TIME OF MINISTRY

Pray for your students that through these levels of prayer they may experience not only God's presence, but also the answers to their prayers.

EVALUATIONS

A self-evaluation questionnaire may be a good way to evaluate the established student objectives.

RECOMMENDATIONS

Methodological

An excellent method to carry out the development of the subject is through illustration; teach using graphics or a multimedia presentation for each one of the levels of prayer.

STUDENTS' ASSIGNMENT

Use the model prayer both individually and with your family, keeping in mind each of its levels. Attend at least one intercession service a week.

5 Questionnaire for Further Study

1. Write down four ways in which we can draw near God, Hebrews 10:22.

_____

_____

_____

_____

2. Complete with the correct answers, Luke 11:9.

Ask and

_____

Seek and

_____

Knock and

_____

3. Which are the three requirements we must meet while praying? Matthew 6:5-7.

1 _____
2 _____
3 _____

4. In your own words, tell how the Lord's Prayer is significant to you.

_____

_____

_____

_____

5. Fill in the blanks, Philippians 4:6.

Do not _____ about _____
but in _____ by _____ and _____
with _____, present your _____

_____

6. Copy these verses.

Jeremiah 33:3_____

_____

Psalm 32:5_____

_____

Psalm 23:1_____

_____

Psalm 88:13_____

_____

Matthew 21:22_____

_____

Acts 2:42_____

_____

James 5:13_____

_____

7. Complete the sentences from Psalm 34.

I will extol the Lord

_____

His praise

_____

My soul will boast

_____

I sought the Lord

_____

Those who look to Him

_____

This poor man called

_____

The angel of the Lord

_____

Taste and see

_____

The lions may grow weak and hungry

_____

I will teach you

_____

Keep your tongue

_____

Turn from

_____

The eyes of the Lord are

_____

His ears

_____

The righteous cry out

_____

No one will be condemned

_____

8. What are the three groups of people we must pray for
   according to 1 Timothy 2:1-4?

_____

_____

_____

9. Write down three ways of praying. Ephesians 6:18.

    1._____

    2._____

    3._____

10. What do we have to ask God for concerning preaching the gospel? Ephesians 6:19

_____

_____

11. What must we do every day? Psalm 37:5

_____

_____

Baptism

LESSON

TEACHING OBJECTIVE

The student should understand the importance of water baptism for the new believer and make the decision to obey this commandment.

STUDENT OBJECTIVE

1   The student will mention the significance, the requirements and the benefits of being baptized in water.

2   The student will explain the biblical foundation and the importance of water baptism.

BIBLICAL FOUNDATIONAL REFERENCE

Matthew 28:19

CORRESPONDING BIBLICAL FOUNDATION

Matthew 3:7-8

Mark 1:3-5

Luke 12: 50

Acts 8:15

Acts 19:6

Romans 6:3

Acts 2:37-41

Romans 6:4

KEY TEXT

"Therefore go and make disciples
of all nations, baptizing them in
the name of the Father and of the
Son and of the Holy Spirit"
(Matthew 28:19)

We can say that in the New Testament we find references concerning 4 types of baptism.

1. The Baptism of John the Baptist

It was performed during the time of the preparation of the way for Jesus (Matthew 3:7-9 and Mark 1:3-5). It took place in Jordan where the multitudes headed. It is mentioned over and over again as Baptism of Repentance. John encouraged the ones being baptized to show their repentance and to confess their sins. He also encouraged the people to believe in the one who would come after him: Jesus Christ, of whom he gave testimony.

At the time Jesus was baptized, He was anointed by the Holy Spirit for the beginning of His ministry and it was the time when he received witness of how pleased the Father was.

2. The Baptism of Suffering of Jesus

This indicates that God baptized Jesus in the sins and sicknesses of man in order to make Him upright and righteous (Luke 12:50).

3. The Christian's baptism in water

Acts 2:38

4. The Christian's baptism in the Holy Spirit

Acts 8:15, Acts 19:6

A. Definition

Baptism comes from the original Greek word "baptizo" and the root "bapto" means to wet or submerge; this can only be accomplished by submerging the person totally in water. This act should be performed by a person of spiritual authority, such as the pastor, deacon, or leader who has been granted such authority (Romans 6:3).

-Baptizo is the intensive form of "BAPTIEN" which means to submerge.

-In baptism the idea expressed is the union of someone or something.

-Baptism is part of the Great Commission (Matthew 28:19).

-We identify ourselves with Christ in His death, His burial and His resurrection (Romans 6:4).

-It is a public confession that states we are dead with Christ to our sins.

B. Importance of Water Baptism

The first thing we should understand is that it is a commandment which implies identifying yourself with Christ as Lord, with His death and His resurrection to a new life. Additionally, being baptized makes us disciples of Jesus.

"He who says he abides in Him ought himself also to walk just as He walked" (I John 2:6).

At the age of 30 Jesus descended into the waters of Baptism. This was the first experience of his public ministry. John hesitated to baptize Jesus and said:

"I have need to be baptized by you, and are you coming to me? But Jesus answered and said to him, "Permit it to be so now, for thus it is fitting for us to fulfill all righteousness" (Matthew 3:14-15).

Though Jesus did not need to go through the baptism of repentance of John because he had not committed sin nor was their deceit in his mouth, he did it to give us the example of obedience and confirm that this was the requirement established by God for justification. In 1 Peter 2:24 it says Christ gave us examples in all things in order for us to follow in his steps.

We should be baptized in water because:

- We are disciples of Christ. I John 2:6.
- Christ gave us the example. Matthew 3:14-15.
- It is a step of obedience by faith. James 2:17-18.

C. Requirements for being baptized

By being baptized in water we give public testimony that all of our sins have been washed by the blood of Christ and have been buried with his death to walk in a new life. To reach this experience that comes after repentance and the confession of our faith in Christ, it is necessary to fulfill various requirements.

Believe

Belief comes before baptism; no one can be baptized unless he has believed before. In Mark 16:16 the Lord Jesus says, "Whoever believes and is baptized will be saved but whoever does not believe will be condemned" (Mark 16:16).

Recognize the work of the cross

The belief of the person to be baptized is linked to the knowledge of the sacrifice of Christ on the cross of Calvary as the only way to redemption. Notice the case of the Ethiopian; he manifests his conviction clearly saying: "I believe Jesus Christ is the Son of God" (Acts 8:37). It is understood that by saying this he did not only believe in Jesus but also in his work of the Cross.

Bring fruit worthy of repentance

Simon the magician believed in Philip's message, he repented and was baptized. When the multitudes went to John the Baptist to be baptized he would say "O generation of vipers! Who warned you to flee from the wrath to come?

"Bring fruit worthy of repentance ..." (Luke 3:7-8).

John leads us to understand that repentance and baptism go together. It is necessary to demonstrate the fruit of repentance. But when asked, "What should we do ?" He responds by saying he who has two tunics give one to whoever doesn't have and he who has food to eat to the same thing.

In Acts 2:38 we find this again when Peter finishes his speech to the Jews saying:

"Repent and be baptized in the name of Jesus Christ for the remission of sins and you shall receive the gift of the Holy Spirit." To summarize we can say that the steps prior to baptism are: Believing the message of the word, recognizing Christ's sacrifice on the cross, manifesting it by the confession of our faith. This makes us realize that it is impossible for infants to be baptized for they are not in the capacity of understanding the commitment that they are up to take part in.

D. Benefits of being baptized

Three significant steps in baptism:

1.The heavens open

This means that our relationship with God becomes more direct. Baptism gives us the right to have a constant, personal relationship with the Lord. Our prayers get to his divine presence without any obstacles.

2. The Holy Spirit comes upon your life

The Holy Spirit comes to cloth your inner man of Christ. The Scriptures say:
"For all of you who were baptized into Christ have clothed yourselves with Christ"
(Galatians 3:27).

3. The voice of God comes to the heart

Like with Jesus, every person that experiences the baptism of water has the opportunity to hear the Father say: "You are my son, whom I love; with you I am well pleased,"through these words God wants us to know that when we come down to the waters willing to give up our old nature, He is filled with great joy and He starts seeing us as His children. It is interesting to note that Jesus received the Fullness of the Holy Spirit in his life after having been baptized.

CONCLUSION

We should be baptized for as followers of Christ we walk according to his example. He was not sprinkled with water but was totally submerged. He ordained it and the apostles guided by this, taught and did the same (Acts 2:37-41).

APPLICATION

In our Christian life it is important to fulfill this commandment and it is fundamental that we understand the importance baptism has. If you have not done so yet, get baptized; and if you have already done so, explain its importance to others.

EVALUATION

Ask some students to come to the front and explain the importance, the benefits and the requirements to be baptized.

RECOMMENDATIONS

Biblical

It is necessary to be acquainted with the Scriptures that speak about Baptism in water.

Read the book "Submerged in His Spirit" by Pastor Cesar Castellanos

Methodological

Work in groups and have the student do a deeper research on this subject. All should participate.

STUDENTS' ASSIGNMENT

Each student should be baptized before level one is complete.

6 Questionnaire for Further Study

1.   What does the word baptism mean? _____
_____

2.   Give one reason Jesus was baptized. _____
_____

3.   What is the importance of the baptism?
a. _____
b. _____
c. _____

4.   What are the requirements needed to be baptized?
_____

5.   Explain at least two benefits for being baptized. _____
_____

6. Find three scriptures where baptism is mentioned and its
characteristics: _____
_____

Faith

TEACHING OBJECTIVE

The student must understand the biblical concept of faith and its significance for a growing and victorious life.

STUDENT OBJECTIVE

1   The student must define the concept of faith in a biblical and theoretical way.

2   The student must give a clear explanation of the different kinds of faith.

Hebrews 11:1-41

CORRESPONDING BIBLICAL FOUNDATION

Genesis 15:6

Psalm 55:22

Psalm 57:1

Job 13:15

Isaiah 40:31

Luke 5:4,5

Isaiah 1:19,20

1 Peter 1:7

KEY TEXT

"Now faith is being sure of what we hope for and certain of what we do not see... And without faith it is impossible to please God, because anyone who comes to him must believe that He exists and that He rewards those who earnestly seek him" **(Hebrews 11:1, 6).**

PURPOSE

"The spiritual environment of this city is quite difficult. People don't want to get involved in the things of God." Those were the words of one of the pastors who came to welcome me at the airport of a city in Canada. My response to that comment was, "The problem is not in the people, but in you." Then I told him of an anecdote Dr. Norman Vincent Peale used to tell. Once when he was in China, Dr. Peale visited a tattoo parlor. While he was there the phrase "born-to-lose" caught his attention so he asked one of the parlor attendants, "would someone actually have those words tattooed onto their skin?" The Chinese man told him that some people do indeed. "I can not believe it!" he thought but Dr. Peale's greatest surprise came when the attendent tattoo told him that, before a person gets something like that tattooed onto their body, they have already tattooed it into their mind.

Looking straight in the pastor's eyes, I told him, "If you think that it is difficult for people in this city to accept the things of God, that will be the result but, if you believe you will be able to reach them through the gospel, then you will see the fruit of your faith."

I once heard a speaker who said that what we think about during the first five minutes after we wake up, determines the course of our day. Psychologists assert that the first five years of the life of the human being extremely influence the direction of his destiny. Due to the negative experiences many people have lived through, some have allowed the enemy to tattoo "Born-to-lose" or "You-are-a-failure" in their minds. On the cross of Calvary the Lord Jesus Christ erased any stamp that the enemy has printed onto our lives. Then He re-stamped us with, "You are a child of God" (John 1:12).

This mark or stamp, printed by the very Holy Spirit in our hearts, gives us legal rights over the circumstances, since we have become part of God's family.

This lesson will help you to know the principles of a victorious faith, and you will find the elements to stir up in your heart.

1.FAITH MAKES US CONQUERORS

No child of God is a failure because even when we have to face different adversities, in Christ we are more than conquerors. You decide what kind of faith you are going to have. John said, "For everyone born of God overcomes the world." This is the victory that has overcome the world, even our faith" (1 John 5:4).
Who overcomes the world? The one who believes that Jesus is the Son of God.

When the aged Policarpo was carried to the roman circus to be judged because of his faith in Jesus Christ, the proconsul told him, "Curse Christ and I will give you back your freedom!" Policarpo answered, "I have served him for 86 years and He has never harmed me so how could I curse my King and Savior? Since you seem to ignore who I am, I will be frank with you, I am a Christian."

He was not afraid of the emperor's wrath, or of the crowd who violently cried out, "Burn him!, burn him!" He was not afraid of the wild beasts, or the stake, or death, because for him Christ was the all in all.

A. By Faith we overcome the world

The apostle John said: "We know that we are children of God and that the whole world is under the control of the evil one." (1 John 5:19) There are evil powers in the air that try to control and manipulate individuals, families, businesses, political arenas and the church world at large etc... That is why it is necessary to develop an active faith that is able to bring the presence of God to our families and to our cities and nations.

The apostle Paul wrote to the Corinthians: "For though we live in the world, we do not wage war as the world does. The weapons we fight with are not the weapons of the world. On the contrary, they have divine power to tear down strongholds. We demolish arguments and every high thing that sets itself up against the knowledge of God and we take captive every thought to make it obedient to Christ (2 Corinthians 10:3-5).

B. By faith we overcome every argument against us

The human mind is the enemy's primary target because it is there that faith is developed. He will make every effort to enslave the mind so that we do not take time to consider the ways of God or search out His truths in the scriptures; but as a child of God, we must excercise our spiritual authority, identify this argument and pull down any stronghold the adversary has raised up in our mind. We must cancel every argument that the adversary has used against us, and do it through the power of the cross of Calvary. Any thought that is not of God and any confusion in our minds must be bound and submitted to Jesus' authority.

Even when the whole world is under the enemy's control, we have God's help in that we own the weapons necessary to overcome the enemy and his armies. Paul reminds us that, "greater is He who is in us than the one that is in the world" (1 John 4:4).

Faith is the power that steers a man through his Christian life, his walk. This faith comes when you have an absolute dependence on the Word of God. The Bible says: "faith comes by way of hearing the message, and the message is heard through the word of God" (Romans 10:17). Living the Christian life means that we submit to and obey divine principles. This is how our trust in God increases.

D. L. Moody once said that he used to close his Bible and then ask for faith. Then he realized that to have faith he needed to open his bible and study the Word; since then his faith never stopped growing.

2. DIFFERENT KINDS OF FAITH

A. The creative faith

"By faith we understand that the universe was formed at God's command, so that what is seen was not made out of what was visible" (Hebrews 11:3).

God has endowed us with his own nature, and by faith we call things that are not as though they were. In the same way Abraham believed that God would give him a son, even when circumstances were opposing. Faith has the ability to see what the physical sight cannot see.

Conceiving faith by the word

An angel came to the virgin, Mary, to tell her that she would conceive a child. She believed and did conceive by the Spirit. If a Christian believes God and lets His Word become "rhema" for his life, he will notice that this Word conceives the miracle in the inner part of his being and then he will see the results.

B. Faith for healing the soul

"A happy heart makes a cheerful countenance, but heartache crushes the spirit" (Proverbs 15:13).

One area that brings us into the dimension of faith is inner healing or healing of the wounded soul. A special dose of faith is required for the soul of a person to be restored.

C. Faith to give an offering

"By faith Abel offered God a better sacrifice than Cain did. By faith he was commended as a righteous man, when God spoke well of his offerings. And by faith he still speaks, even though he is dead" (Hebrews 11:4).

The Lord honored Abel's faith above Cain's because when Cain also presented an offering, it was not pleasing to God since with it came indifference and selfishness. Cain had not accepted God as his creator. Remember, the faith to offer is the same faith that enriches.

D. Faith for (physical) healing

"Surely he took our infirmities and carried our sorrows, yet we considered him stricken by God, smitten by him, and afflicted. But he was pierced for our transgressions, he was crushed for our iniquities; the punishment that brought us peace was upon him, and by his wounds we are healed" (Isaiah 53:4-5).

Faith is essential for the healing of your body. To obtain it, you must walk in the reality that, whatever ails you, has already been conquered by Jesus Christ on the cross.

3. CHARACTERISTICS OF FAITH

All along the Scriptures we can find a broad list of features that emphasize faith as a gift of God.

The following are some of them:

- Faith believes in the words of the Lord (Luke 5:4-5)

- Faith is above the senses (Isaiah 1:19-20)

- Faith overcomes the doubts and unbelief (1 Peter 1:7)

CONCLUSION

Faith is absolute trust that the believer places in God and in each one of His promises. It allows him to declare things that are not as if they already are. Faith is an agent that, unlike hope, operates in the present and is the main requirement that God demands of us in order to approach Him. It operates in all the areas of our lives, helping us to experience the supernatural.

APPLICATION

What emblem do you have printed in your mind? Remember that as a child of God the Lord printed "born to succeed" in your heart.

Try to diligently take care of every thought that goes into your mind. Set out, deliberately, in your heart not to accept a single negative thought during a whole day. Once you achieved it, extend it for a week, then a month. You will notice that all the thoughts in your mind come from the Spirit of God.

TIME OF MINISTRY

Ask God to renew the faith of your students so that they may not faint in difficult situations. Pray that God will strengthen them to overcome.

EVALUATION

A self-evaluation questionnaire may be a good tool to use to find out how well the students understand and apply the steps for a victorious life that we established in the lessons.

RECOMMENDATIONS

Bibliographical

In order to achieve a better development of the subject, it is necessary to read the book, Entering the Dimension of Faith from the series, As Firm As The Rock, by Pastor Cesar Castellanos.

Biblical

Display significant biblical verses related to the subject. For example, Genesis 15:6; 1 Peter 1:7. This may be a good memorizing exercise.

Methodological

We recommend question and answer time for students so that we can access the level of faith of each student.

STUDENTS´ ASSIGNMENT

Students can research two different cases in the Bible portraying true faith and lack of faith. This way you will be able to determine if the subject was fully understood. Review the STUDENTS´ ASSIGNMENT upon the following class.

7 Questionnaire for Further Study

1. The word faith appears about 128 times in the New Testament. Select six texts about faith that had an impact on your life and explain why.

A._____ Because _____
B._____ Because _____
C._____ Because _____
D._____ Because _____
E._____ Because _____
F._____ Because _____

2. Hebrews 11: 6 Faith is a condition to _____ and believe that He exists, and He _____.

3. 2 Corinthians 5:7 we live by _____, and not by _____
_____

4. Define the following terms found in Hebrews 11:1

certainty
_____
_____

Conviction_____
_____

5. Based on Hebrews 11, write down what happened to these people as they were led by faith:

ABEL
_____

ENOCH
_____

NOAH

_____

ABRAHAM

_____

SARAH

_____

ISAAC

_____

JACOB

_____

JOSEPH

_____

MOSES

_____

RAHAB (the prostitute)

_____

6. When the angel visited Mary telling her that she had been chosen to be Jesus' mother, she uttered an expression that summarizes her belief and acceptance by faith. What was this expression? (Luke 1:38).

_____

_____

7. Complete the following text that expresses in concrete terms Peter's act of faith:
"When he had finished speaking, he said to Simon, _____

_____

Simon answered, 'Master, we've worked hard all night and

_____

(Luke 5:4-5).

8. Some invisible powers work to weaken our faith through unbelief but the apostle John teaches something about it. Explain it in your own words (1 John 5: 10).

_____

_____

_____

_____

9. Faith is a distinctive element of the spiritual warrior. Describe the other details that make up the armor of God according to Ephesians 6: 10-18.

_____

10. Match the following texts with the corresponding acts of faith:

A. The man with a shriveled hand   Mark 5: 28,29 ( )
B. The paralytic of Capernaum   Mark 7: 26-30 ( )
C. Jairus' daughter   Matthew 12: 13 ( )
D. The Syrophoenician woman   Luke 8:40-42; 50 ( )
E. The woman that touched the robe   Mark 2:11,12 ( )

The Holy Spirit

TEACHING OBJECTIVE

The student must understand the significance of being filled with the Holy Spirit and the necessary principles to obtain and keep this experience.

STUDENT OBJECTIVE

1   The student must be able to explain the necessary steps in order to receive the infilling of the Holy Spirit.

2   The student must be able to describe the Holy Spirit using biblical references.

BIBLICAL FOUNDATIONAL
REFERENCE

John 14:15-26

Acts 1:7-9

CORRESPONDING
BIBLICAL
FOUNDATION

Acts 2:1-23

Ephesians 1:11-14

Acts 10:38

John 16:14-15

John 3:1-15

John 16:13

1 Corinthians 2:9,10

KEY TEXT

"But the Counselor, the Holy
Spirit, whom the Father will
send in my name, will teach you
all things and will remind you of
everything I have said to you."
(John 14:26)

PURPOSE

"Lord, how can I know that I did not make a mistake. How can I know that I am not with the wrong group of people?" This was part of my prayer a few days after I was converted to Christianity. Even though I was on my knees at the altar of a small church, I had many doubts. I had already read enough of the Bible to know that I could ask the Lord for signs. So I did just that. I prayed, "Lord, if you are indeed in this, I ask, as a sign, that you allow me to see you. I ask, Lord, that you lay your hands on my head and anoint me."

Before I had finished my prayer, I felt the presence of a person behind me. In my spirit I turned around to look and I saw the stature of a glorious being, dressed in white. Slowly, I lifted my eyes because I so longed to see His face. But when I did, I experienced something similar to what it's like for someone who has spent a long time in darkness and suddenly opens his eyes to the brightness of a new sunny morning; the impact of the brightness was so strong that the eyes could not withstand it, no matter how hard you try. So that's how it is when trying to look upon the beauty of the face of the Lord. Our eyes are still not prepared to stand such brilliance. When I saw him, all the strength of my body vanished and I fell to the floor as a dead man.

The Lord bowed down and laid his hands on my head. In that moment I felt that my entire being was filling up with a powerful glory coming from the very presence of God. Then, I began to speak in a language I did not understand, then in another one, then in yet another one and so on. I spoke in about seven different languages. But for me, this was not the most important thing. Knowing that God was within me and that I could feel Him, was.

When I got up from my knees I began to jump and run for joy embracing everybody. In my excitement I exclaimed, "God is in me!" Unfortunately, this was unfamiliar to the rest of the people. Nobody in that church understood me. My family actually thought that I was experiencing an emotional breakdown of sorts and considered it to be indicative of my age! But on the inside I knew that I would never be the same because the Holy Spirit of God was dwelling in me and that was the only thing that mattered.

When we become Christians and develop a genuine, permanent relationship with the Father, Son and Holy Spirit, the best privileges of life are ours to enjoy.

In John 20:22 we read, "And with that he breathed on them and said, 'Receive the Holy Spirit.'" Receiving the Holy Spirit is receiving the seal of the promise that guarantees we are children of God.

For the Lord Jesus it was very important that each one of his followers would learn to walk with the Holy Spirit. He, being God incarnate, needed the presence of the Spirit in order to successfully develop the STUDENT'S ASSIGNMENT that the Father had given him. The absence of the Holy Spirit in the life of the believer equals to having a body without a spirit. The Spirit of God must be the most important thing for the Christian because, without Him, the believer will not be able to develop the full potential assigned to him by his Creator. When the believer allows the Holy Spirit to take control, then the Spirit is like an indelible seal in his life, distinguishing him as a Christian anointed by the power of God.

In this lesson the student will begin to know this interesting person of the Trinity. More importantly, the student will experience the need to establish a friendship with Him, understanding that it is about the presence of God in his life.

1. DEEPENING YOUR KNOWLEDGE OF THE HOLY SPIRIT

We all must obtain complete knowledge of who the Holy Spirit is and understand his work. The following features help to identify him in a better way:

a. He is a person

The Holy Spirit is a person as real as the Lord Jesus Christ is. He is the third person of the Trinity. Jesus was completely confident that He could accurately represent him. That is the reason why Jesus gave this promise to his disciples. However, he is a person to whom the world can neither see no receive because the Holy Spirit of God is only given to those who acknowledge Jesus as their Lord and Savior.

The following reasons help us to confirm that the Holy Spirit is a person:

- He speaks (Acts 13:2; John 16:13)
- He leads and warns (Acts 16:6,7)
- He offers help and intercedes (Romans 8: 26)
- He guides (Romans 8:14; John 16:13)
- He testifies (John 15:26)
- He grieves or is saddened (Ephesians 4:30)

b. He is God Himself

The Holy Spirit has been at work from the moment of creation up until this very moment. His attributes allow us to identify him as God himself. The following verses give us direction regarding this: Luke 1:35; Psalm 139:7; Hebrews 9:14; 1 Corinthians 2:10-11

c. He glorifies Jesus

Everything the Holy Spirit does glorifies Jesus. When a person stops glorifying Jesus with his actions, his words, etc. the Holy Spirit stands still. If we have a close friendship with Him, we will have direct access to the divine treasures and the third person of the Trinity will be in charge of helping us enjoy them. In other words, our faith in Jesus Christ gives us the legal rights to His riches but our relationship with the Spirit allows us to enjoy them. When we glorify Jesus through our actions the Spirit rejoices and increases His power in us. (John 16:14-15; John 7:38-39)

d. Causes us to be born again

It is only by the Holy Spirit that we can be considered children of God, since it is His work that allows us to be born again. Don't forget Nicodemus´ question about the new birth and the Lords' response in John 3:5-6. In order to be born of the Spirit of God it is necessary to die first; that is, if a person does not die to sin the Spirit will not bring new life to him.

e. He is our Guide

When Jesus was on the earth He said I am the way, and the truth, and the life.... He was and continues to be the only way to the Father but while leaving, Jesus promised to send the Holy Spirit to guide us so that we do not abandon the right path (John 16:13). He is the one who can perfectly interpret the map of the Word of God and as Jesus said, it will guide us into all truth.

The person who does not cultivate an intimate relationship with the Holy Spirit might be at risk of doctrinal deviation.

f. He reveals the divine secrets

The Father and the Son share the infinite riches of their grace but they are clearly revealed to us through the Holy Spirit. As an authorized steward of those blessings, those riches, and all the divine secrets, the Holy Ghost imparts them to those that, by faith, have surrendered to Jesus and are filled with the Holy Spirit. (Deuteronomy 29:29; 1 Corinthians 2:9-10)

2. STEPS TO RECEIVE THE INFILLING OF THE HOLY SPIRIT

a. Cleanliness of heart

The Lord said: "And no one pours new wine into old wineskins" (Luke 5:37). The wine represents the fresh and vigorous presence of the Holy Spirit that wants to be poured out in completely regenerated lives. The old wineskins represent those persons who experienced the presence of the Spirit in their lives for a moment, but due to several circumstances, lost their communion (relationship) with God. The new wineskin is the life that has been completely transformed by God (2 Corinthians 5:17).

b. Believe

In the Christian life, we walk in faith and through faith. When we ask for the baptism of the Holy Spirit, we must accept in faith that we already have it and then begin, in that same attitude of faith, speaking to the Lord in new tongues. If a person is filled with God he will express it with his words. On the contrary, if he is filled with hatred and bitterness, he will use his words to show that as well, because the mouth expresses evidence of what is in the heart (Matthew 12:34).

c. Do not yield the body to sin

We must constantly remember that the Holy Spirit is the presence of God in our lives. Paul, the apostle indicates this in 1 Corinthians 3:16. Don't you know that you yourselves are God's temple and that God's Spirit lives in you? This text implies that God has chosen our body as the dwelling place of His Spirit and He cannot dwell in a house contaminated with sin (See Romans 6:13 and James 3:8-12).

d. Receive Him Voluntarily

The Holy Spirit is a gentleman. He only enters a person's life when the person willingly decides to invite him to come in and when this happens He enters to take over every area of their being, offering power and absolute freedom (2 Corinthians 3:17).

CONCLUSION

The Holy Spirit is the third person of the Trinity (Father, Son and Holy Spirit), and He is the promise given by Jesus to his disciples made reality, being the Comforter, He indicated that He would send it as soon as He departed. The Spirit of God comes to dwell in the life of the believer as his friend and guide, to endow him with power and take over every area of his life.

APPLICATION

Make sure that the Holy Spirit is guiding your life. Examine your daily life and observe, according to your behavior and accomplishments if you really are accompanied by the Holy Spirit as taught in these lessons.

TIME OF MINISTRY

As the teacher, you must evaluate the group to see if there are some students who have allowed the Holy Spirit to be extinguished from their lives. Dedicate time to pray for them in order to revive the Spirit again; pray for those who have not yet received the evidence of speaking in tongues as well.

EVALUATION

Emphasize all points covered in this class in order to evaluate the objectives. Highlight the main characteristic of the Holy Spirit, that he is A PERSON. Then review the features of a person filled with the Holy Spirit.

RECOMMENDATIONS

Bibliographical

In order to achieve a better development of the subject, it is necessary to read the book, Immersed in His Spirit, from the series As Firm As The Rock, by Pastor Cesar Castellanos.

Biblical

Ephesians 4:23-32 provides the characteristics of the fullness of the Holy Spirit.

Methodological

We recommend questions and answers in order to know if the students are understanding and applying what is being taught. During the class take time to clarify any doubts that the students may have.

STUDENTS' ASSIGNMENT

Examine every area in your life and point out which areas are controlled by the Holy Spirit. If you find any weak area, take time to ask the Holy Spirit to fill you in order to establish a more intimate communion with Him.

8 Questionnaire for Further Study

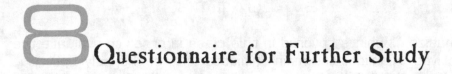

1. According to Acts 2:4, the evidence of the demonstration that the ones in the upper room had been filled with the Holy Spirit was:

A. A healing miracle.
B. Speaking in other tongues.
C. An increase of communion.
D. All of the above.
E. None of the above.

2. What did the crowd assume when they got to the upper room and saw the people? (Acts 2:7-12).

_____

3. In his first speech, Peter made reference to the prophecy spoken by (Acts 2:16-21) _____. Express the content of this prophecy emphasizing what God said He would do:

_____
_____
_____

4. According to Acts 2:37-41 which were the conditions that Peter stated to those present, to receive the Holy Spirit?

_____

How many people were converted through Peter's message?

_____

5. From each text, give specific examples of the work of the Holy Spirit in us:

Ephesians 1: 13   The Holy Spirit....

_____
_____

1 Timothy 4:1 The Holy Spirit...

_____

_____

Romans 5:5   The Holy Spirit...

_____

_____

Acts 1:8 The Holy Spirit fills us with _____
and makes us _____

_____

John 14: 26   The Holy Spirit...
_____ all things.

John 16:8   The Holy Spirit _____ in
regards to sin and righteousness and judgment.

John 16:13   The Holy Spirit ...
_____ into all truth.

6. According to Matthew 3:11 We will be baptized with

_____

and with _____ .

7. Read Acts 19: 1-6 and check with an "X" the right order of
actions between Paul and the disciples in Ephesus:

a. Baptism in the name of Jesus,
       ( ) Laying on of hands,
       ( ) Filled with the Holy Spirit,
       ( ) Speaking in tongues and prophesying,

b. Filled with the Holy Spirit,
       ( ) Laying on of hands,
       ( ) Speaking in tongues and prophesying,
       ( ) Baptism in the name of Jesus,

8. According to Romans 8:26, when communicating with God,
what is the work of the Spirit on our behalf and how does He do
it?
_____

Laying on of Hands

LESSON

TEACHING OBJECTIVE

The student must understand how the power of God flows through laying on of hands.

STUDENT OBJECTIVE

1 The student must be able to explain the significance of the laying on of hands as it relates to ministering to others.

2 The student must be able to explain the purposes for the laying on of hands.

3 The student must give three suggestions for not acting hastily when laying hands.

BIBLICAL FOUNDATIONAL REFERENCE

1 Timothy 5:21-22

2 Timothy 1:6-7

CORRESPONDING BIBLICAL FOUNDATION

Exodus 15:6-7

Exodus 15:12-13

Genesis 48:11-20

Matthew 11:2-5

Mark 5:21-23; 35-42

Mark 5:24-34

Acts 9:10-12

Acts 13:1-3

Proverbs 28:3

John 12:24

KEY TEXT

"For this reason I remind you to
fan the flame of the gift of God,
which is in you through the
laying on of my hands"
(2 Timothy 1:6)

PURPOSE

An important aspect in the development of the Christian life is the disposition of the believer to grow in the knowledge of biblical doctrine with the purpose of remaining firm in the ways of God and at the same time count on the sufficient authority to help others in spiritual matters. The basic doctrines you should know can be found in Hebrews 6:1-2. In this text it mentions the imposition of hands, as a fundamental doctrine the church should not be careless about it.

Through the laying on of hands, which implies physical contact, the Lord Jesus Christ performed countless miracles throughout His ministry. Also, the apostle Paul made sure that Timothy was informed of its significance, pointing out how careful he should be while practicing it.

Applying this doctrine with the knowledge and the delegated authority established by God, a person can be used to minister blessings from Above to others. But, if this practice is performed out of biblical context, the opposite could take place.

The purpose of this lesson is to help you understand in a clear manner not only what is involved in the laying on of hands but to offer you the necessary tools according to the biblical context and the examples of Jesus permitting you to be a genuine instrument in the hands of God to minister to others.

1. WHAT DO WE MEAN BY LAYING ON OF HANDS?

It is one of the basic doctrines of the Christian faith. It is an act whereby a person in spiritual authority, lays his hands on another in order to impart blessings, together with prayer and prophesy.

This definition implies, then, that if the person who lays on his hands is not in an adequate spiritual condition, he will not be a channel for blessings; by which we infer that we must be ministered to before, in order to minister to others.

According to Psalm 119:73 and Job 10:8-9 we can say that laying on of hands is a means God uses to give life.

2. BIBLICAL PROOF OF THE PRACTICE OF THIS DOCTRINE

a. In the Old Testament

God used His right hand to work precisely during the creation. He does so as well when constantly leading his people, blessing them, performing miracles, bringing provision and causing the impossible. The following are examples of laying on of hands as recorded in the Old Testament:

- Jacob blesses Ephraim and Manasseh (Genesis 48:11-20).

Being of old age, Jacob wanted to bless Joseph's sons. The blessing was like a heritage that the father passed to the new generations and it always came to the one who was ON the right hand (Genesis 48:24).

- Moses anoints his successor (Deuteronomy 34).

From the moment that Moses was called, God told him that his purpose was to set the people free. But, when he arrived at the border of Canaan, the Lord told him to let Joshua take over and he would now lead the people into the Promised Land. (Numbers 27:18-23)

b.   New Testament

- In the New Testament, laying on of hands is emphasized in the ministry of the Lord Jesus.

In Matthew 11:2-5 we read about the works that Jesus Christ performed on earth under the authority of His Father God. He did it by laying his hands, releasing the anointing poured out on him by the Holy Spirit (Luke 4:18-21).

Afterwards, based on his own experience and acknowledging the power in the laying on of hands, Paul supported his ministry with signs and wonders performed in the same way (Acts 14:3).

3. PURPOSES OF LAYING ON OF HANDS

It is practiced for various purposes:

A. To impart inner healing and deliverance

Inner healing and deliverance are two stages that every individual has to go through if he desires to be used by God and live the Christian life in abundance. The Lord Jesus himself was anointed to bring inner healing and deliverance, according to what He himself said in Luke 4:18. In this text, the broken-hearted are all those who need healing for their wounded soul. And the prisoners are those who are oppressed by unclean spirits.

B. To impart blessing

In Genesis 48:13-20, the story of Ephraim and Manasseh reminds us of the way laying on of hands was done in ancient times. It was a sign of blessing. In Mark 10:16 we see a similar case in Jesus' time, when He took the children in his arms, put his hands on them and blessed them.

C. To impart authority

Let us not forget the process of the transfer of authority from Moses to Joshua based on the order given by God, through the laying on of hands. Another similar case happened to Elisha, who laid his hands on Jehoash, king of Israel (2 Kings 13:15-17).

D. To impart physical healing

The spirit of sickness, like every unclean spirit, can be defeated through laying on of hands in the name of Jesus (Matthew 16:17-18; James 5:14-15). Laying on of hands encourages peoples´ faith; who ever ministers by this practice must do it in a dimension of absolute faith.

E. To impart the baptism of the Holy Spirit

God's purpose for every believer is that he experiences the fullness of the Holy Spirit and has an intimate relationship with Him. As we have already studied, the Holy Spirit is Jesus' promise fulfilled, to the disciples (Luke 24:49b). He is God's power working in our lives (Acts 1:8), and His anointing comes to us through the laying on of hands (Acts 8:18).

F. To impart gifts and commission people

We have studied about the gifts of the Holy Spirit and according to the Scriptures, they can be imparted by laying on of hands. In Romans 1:11 Paul says, I long to

see you so that I may impart to youre spiritual gifts.... In his book, The Spirit Filled Believer Handbook, Dr. Derek Prince affirms that a believer has the authority, according to the scriptures, to impart spiritual gifts to another (1 Timothy 4:14, 2 Timothy 1:6).
Likewise, laying on of hands is used to impart authority for someone to perform a specific STUDENTS´ ASSIGNMENT in the work of ministry. Remember that Barnabas and Saul were set apart for the work and by order of the Holy Spirit, through laying on of hands (Acts 13:1-4).

CONCLUSION

Laying on of hands is included as part of doctrinal basics for Christian living. As stated before, it is the act by which a person in authority imparts blessings to another person. However, this puts a demand on the one who is ministering to be in the very best spiritual condition so that they do not yield an opposing effect to God's purpose in the life of the one being ministered to.

Through the laying on of hands, the Lord imparts life and a significant blessing that brings deliverance and inner healing to the person that has confessed his faith in Jesus Christ.

APPLICATION

Do an in depth study on what can be attained through the laying on of hands, and prepare yourself spiritually for the Lord to use you as a channel to bless others.

TIME OF MINISTRY

Pray to God for your students to become sensitive to hearing God's voice so that they can minister to others.

EVALUATION

A self-evaluation questionnaire or a paper written on this subject may be good tools to use to gauge the students progress. See biblical recommendations.

RECOMMENDATIONS

Bibliographical

In order to better develop the subject it is necessary to read the book, His Hand Is Upon Me, from the series "As Firm As The Rock" by Pastor Cesar Castellanos.

Biblical

The book of Acts provides good examples of the laying on of hands in the ministry of the First Church. A deeper study on the part of the instructor and the student is essential for a better understanding of the subject. It is a good way to assess the fruit from the teaching as well.

Methodological

We suggest that you confer together with your students to develop this lesson thoroughly. The use of charts and graphics should be used as a study guideline.

STUDENTS´ ASSIGNMENT

Do a self-evaluation in all areas of your life and observe the needs you find that are out of order. If you find that there are some areas out of order, you will need to go to your pastor or your immediate leader for ministry and deliverance, by the laying on of hands immediately.

9 Questionnaire for Further Study

1. From the foundation of the world, God used his own hands to release his creative power. What do the following scriptures say about it?

Psalm 119:73 _____

Job 10: 8, 9 _____

2. List the things that were made by Jehovah's right hand against the enemies of the people of Israel, according to Exodus 15: 6-7.

_____

_____

_____

3. Since ancient times laying on of hands has been used to impart blessing. Keeping in mind the text of Genesis 48: 11-20, answer the following:

Were both the right hand and the left hand able to bless in the same degree?

     Yes _____   No _____

Did the priority of the blessing lie on the first-born?

     Yes _____   No _____

Why did Israel prefer to lay his right hand on Ephraim if he was the youngest child of Joseph?

_____

4. Write down who is blessing whom by the laying on of hands according to each text.

Numbers 27:22-23 _____

2 Kings 13:15-17 _____

Mark 5: 35-42 _____

Acts 9: 10-12_____

5. What happened to Joshua when Moses laid his hands on him?

Deuteronomy 34:9_____

_____

6. With the help of a biblical concordance, list four specific cases in which Jesus laid his hands on someone:

A. _____ Biblical text

_____

B. _____ Biblical text

_____

C. _____ Biblical text

_____

D. _____ Biblical text

_____

7. During the development of his ministry, Paul the apostle frequently practiced the laying on of hands. Match these texts with the specific corresponding cases for each point:

A. On Timothy   Acts 28: 7-9
B. On Publius' father   Acts 19: 2-6
C. On disciples in Ephesus   2 Timothy 1:6

8. Laying on of hands embraces an awesome power. Complete these text that is an example of it:

"And these signs will accompany those who believe:_____
_____; they will speak in new tongues;

_____

_____; and when they drink deadly poison, it will not hurt them at all; they will place_____,
and they will be healed (Mark 16:17-18).

9. In your own opinion, why did Paul suggest to Timothy not to be hasty in the laying on of hands? (1 Timothy 5: 22)

_____

_____

10. According to Luke 4:18, make a summary of Jesus' ministry, in which laying on of hands was an essential factor. He came to:

_____

_____

_____

_____

11. Which of the previous points are related to deliverance and inner healing?

_____

_____

How to Overcome Obstacles

LESSON 10

TEACHING OBJECTIVE

The student must understand what tools he should use when facing obstacles in his Christian life and how to overcome them.

STUDENT OBJECTIVE

1 The student must be able to explain how to overcome the hindrances that the world may place in his way.

2 The student must be able to explain what proper attitude to have when facing the obstacles.

BIBLICAL FOUNDATIONAL REFERENCE

Romans 8: 35-39

CORRESPONDING BIBLICAL FOUNDATION

John 16:33;

John 17:15-16;

Philippians 4:8;

Romans 8:5-6;

2 Corinthians:14-16;

Psalm 119:9;

James 5: 19-20;

Matthew 26:41;

Matthew 10:36

KEY TEXT

"And, in all these things we are more than conquerors through Him who loved us" **(Romans 8:37).**

PURPOSE

What would you do if you were in the midst of the sea in a small boat being tossed about by powerful waves and raging winds, struggling with all your might to ensure your safety, much to no avail? Such was the predicament of the disciples, according to the story we find in Mathew 8:23-27. Jesus was with them in that same boat, but He was not distressed or afflicted. On the contrary, he was quietly sleeping, as if He were testing how the disciples would react facing adversity.

The experience the apostles lived through is a model lesson for each one of us to hold standard since we all have to encounter difficult situations that will actually help to shape our character. Regardless of the circumstance, we have to remain steadfast and faithful to our divine purpose. Great men of God were fashioned by the fiery tests of difficult times.

Since one of the most frequently asked questions pertains to overcoming obstacles, this lesson will serve as a valuable resource to answer them specifically.

1. THE MOST COMMON OBSTACLES
THE BELIEVER MUST FACE

A. THE WORLD

My prayer is not that you take them out of the world but that you protect them from the evil one. They are not of the world, even as I am not of it (John 17:15-16).

When Jesus prayed for his disciples, He asked God to protect them from the evil that they would have to face in the world. He was well aware of the obstacles that awaited them to throw them off track. When Jesus gave reference to the world, he meant the social systems of our world because they are the things to be used by the enemy as bait to lure Christians into behavior that opposes God's divine order.

In 1 John 2:15-17 we find the description of what the world is and what it can offer us. Things which do not come from the Father, become a hindrance for every believer: the cravings of sinful man, the lust of his eyes and the vain glory of life. Listed are suggestions that help us to overcome the most common obstacles we find in the world:

- Keep your thoughts subject to God's will (Philippians 4:8).
- Dedicate time to the things of the Spirit (Romans 8: 5-6).
- Avoid alliances with the world (2 Corinthians 6:14-16).
- Stay in the Word of God permanently (Psalm 119:9).
- Endeavor to win your acquaintances for the Lord (James 5:19-20)

B. TEMPTATION

"Watch and pray so that you will not fall into temptation. The spirit is willing, but the body is weak" (Matthew 26:41).

In this text we find a special recommendation Jesus gave to his disciples, inviting them to remain in prayer to not give in to daily temptations. It is very important to keep in mind that temptation is a trial from Satan and it is related with the flesh.

Man's sin consists in giving in to that temptation which appears as bait with which the enemy drags man to violate the divine commandments.

You can overcome temptation by:

- Keeping in constant communion with the Spirit through prayer (Luke 11:4; 1 Thessalonians 5:17).
- Study the Word to confess it (Matthew 4).
- Renounce every root of sin that may allow temptations (Proverbs 28:13).
- Fill your mind with things of the Spirit (Galatians 5: 16 y 25).

C. THE FAMILY

For I have come to turn a man against his father, a daughter against her mother, a daughter-in-law against her mother-in-law; a man's enemies will be the members of his own household (Matthew 10:35-36).

For a new believer, it is difficult to suddenly understand that his family could be an obstacle in the development of his Christian life. However, the Lord Jesus warns us about it in the previous text. What we must understand here is that when we accept Jesus as our personal Savior, He must occupy first place in our hearts and only when the whole family enters into that same faith dimension in which we are, will they be able to be in the same spiritual position.

Does this mean that we must argue with our family and be distant from them? Of course not! It is our job to win our family for Christ.

- Win your family through prayer.
- Believe in God's promises.
- Have a good testimony before them.
- Persevere until you win them for Christ.

CONCLUSION

As a rule, man will face several kinds of obstacles that will force him to fight in order to overcome them. These obstacles are like brakes or halts which get in your path, impeding you from reaching a specific goal. In the Christian life there are obstacles placed by the enemy to weaken our faith, but in the hand of God these obstacles turn into key elements to strengthen our character and prepare us to fulfill the work which he has entrusted in us.

TIME OF MINISTRY

Have every student make a list of current obstacles and elaborate on each one of them. Pray for the students for them to renew their faith.

EVALUATION

This can be part of the final exams.

RECOMMENDATIONS

Bibliographical

* Billy Graham's handbook for Christian workers.

* Billy Graham's book, Solutions To the Problems of Life.

Methodological

In order to develop this subject, at the end, the class can be divided into two groups for the purpose of a roleplay demonstration on how to overcome potential obstacles. One student will be in charge of giving a conclusion, related to each area, and the instructor/teacher will remove any doubt they may have.

STUDENTS' ASSIGNMENT

Make a list of those obstacles that you have dealt with throughout your Christian life. Classify the origin i.e. the world, many temptations or your family. Now, take the time to overcome them by applying the suggestions in this lesson.

Select the names of your family members that have not yet met the Lord and claim them for Christ in prayer

10 Questionnaire for Further Study

1. Analyze the text Matthew 8:23-27 and answer the following questions:

A.   What was Jesus doing when the big storm began?

_____

B.   What did the disciples think was going to happen to them in the midst of this problem?

_____

C.   What declaration did Jesus use to exhort the disciples?

_____
_____

D. What did Jesus do in order to get complete calm?

_____
_____

E. What was the men's reaction?

_____

2. In John 16:33 the Lord mentions a key of confidence to face the sorrow of the world. Which is it?

_____
_____

3. Mention some hindrances we find in the world, grouping them according to their rank as described in 1 John 2:15-17:

- Desires of the flesh:

_____
_____

- Lust of the eyes:

_____
_____

- Vain glory of life: _____

_____

4. Temptation is another one of the obstacles present in the believer's life. When Jesus was temped his defense was the proclamation of the Word. Relate each one of Jesus' answers to every attack of the enemy (Matthew 4:1-11).

Satan's attack   Answers of Jesus

"Tell these stones to become bread"...

_____

"If you are the Son of God, throw yourself down"...

_____

"All this I will give you if you will bow down and worship me"...

_____

5. The Beatitudes contain words of encouragement and hope from Jesus to all those that run into trouble (Matthew 5:1-12).

- The word blessed means:

_____

Complete:
- The poor in spirit will receive:

_____

- Those who mourn:

_____

- Those who hunger and thirst for righteousness:

_____

- Those who are persecuted because of righteousness:

_____

_____

6. Paul, the apostle, helps us to understand that since we have difficulties, we must live by faith. 2 Corinthians 4: 8, says that we are:

Pressed on every side, but not

_____

Perplexed, but not

_____

Persecuted, but not

_____

Struck down, but not

_____

7. 2 Corinthians 4:17 For Paul difficulties were a

_____

_____

8. 1 Corinthians 10: 13   Temptation is

_____

     Philippians 4: 13   Strength comes from

_____

     2 Corinthians 1: 6   If we are afflicted

_____

     2 Corinthians 1:20   God's promises are

_____

_____

9. What is the reward for all those who resist temptation? (James 1:12)

_____

10. One of Paul's statements that help us to have courage as we face each difficulty is: (Philippians 4:4)

_____

_____

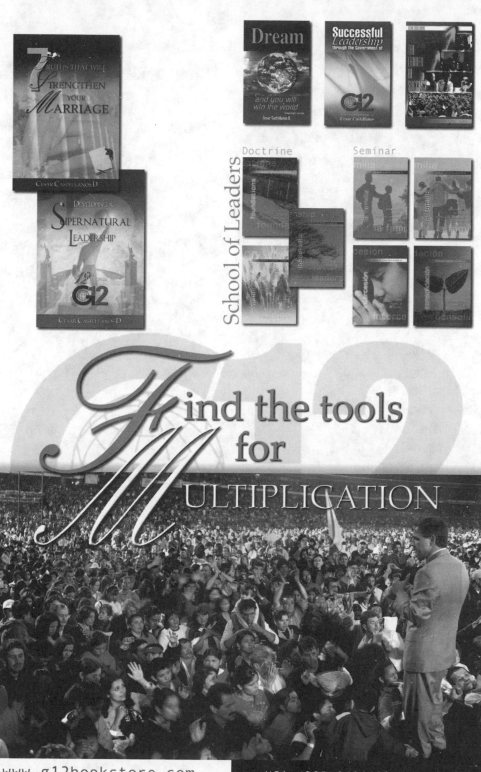